Little People, BIG DREAMS
ARETHA FRANKLIN

Written by
Maria Isabel Sánchez Vegara

Illustrated by
Amy Blackwell

Frances Lincoln
Children's Books

If there was someone in Detroit who was born to sing, it was little Aretha. Her mother was a gospel singer and her father was a preacher who believed that music could move not just people's hearts, but the world.

Her mum left when Aretha was very little, but she never felt alone. Home was always filled with musicians and she learned to play the piano just by listening to them.

She started singing in the gospel choir at the church where her father was a minister. Aretha's voice was so powerful and as smooth as silk. Listening to her, the whole congregation felt that tomorrow would be a brighter day.

Convinced of her talent, Aretha's father took her on tour, and together they went from church to church. Wherever Aretha performed, she did it with such grace that people would cry with joy.

But, even though she loved gospel music, Aretha dreamed that her voice could be heard outside the church, in people's homes. So, when a record company offered her a contract, she didn't have to think about it twice.

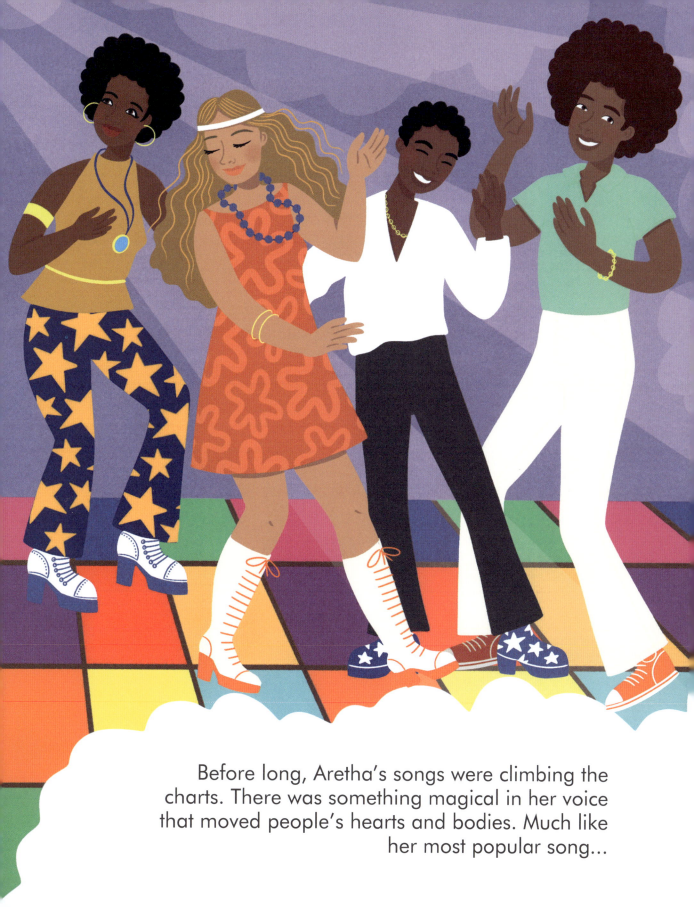

Before long, Aretha's songs were climbing the charts. There was something magical in her voice that moved people's hearts and bodies. Much like her most popular song...

It was called 'Respect', and it was a song written by Otis Redding that sounded brand new in Aretha's voice. Suddenly, the words of a tired working man became an anthem for African American women demanding equal respect.

One of Aretha's friends was Martin Luther King Jr., the great civil rights leader. She stood next to him, challenging people to raise their voices against racism. When he died, she sang the most beautiful song in his honour: 'Precious Lord'.

Aretha started writing her own songs and producing them, too. She went from gospel to jazz, doo-wop and pop, to rhythm and blues... singing every song from the bottom of her heart.

She recorded hundreds of great hits and she loved them all. Aretha used a secret recipe when writing her songs: they had to talk about everyday ups and downs. That's what soul was all about!

ARETHA FRANKLIN

CHUCK BERRY

B.B. KING

ELVIS PRESLEY

It took Aretha 30 long years to be inducted into the Rock & Roll Hall of Fame; she was the first woman in history to be on the list! Aretha was the Queen of Soul and a trailblazer for many other female artists.

But her greatest honour was singing at the inauguration of the first African American president of the United States. Aretha was voicing one of the most important moments in history!

And no-one has ever been able to sing a song quite like Aretha. The little girl who asked for equality and won the R-E-S-P-E-C-T of millions... the greatest soul singer of all time.

ARETHA FRANKLIN

(Born 1942 • Died 2018)

1960

1965

Aretha Franklin was born in Memphis, Tennessee, into a musical family.
The fourth of five children, Aretha understood the power of song at an
early age, joining the congregation at her father's church in joyful, gospel
worship. She was soon a member of the choir, and after her parents
separated, she toured with her father's travelling gospel show. Aretha's
childhood was not without pain and troubles. Her mother, Barbara, left
the family when Aretha was six years old, and died soon afterwards.
Aretha became a mother herself when she was just a teenager, raising
her children in Detroit. But she had dreams beyond the gospel band, and
wanted to share her music more widely as a pop singer. Aged 18, she left
Detroit for the bright lights of New York City. There, she signed a record

1968   2009

deal, creating a string of hit singles that redefined the world of rhythm and blues, with her own style of soul music. Aretha's songs went on to become classics, written from her heart and sung with power and conviction. Aretha's chart dominance soon earned her the title 'Queen of Soul'. At the same time, she became a symbol of black empowerment during the Civil Rights Movement. "Soul to me is a feeling, a lot of depth... being able to bring to the surface that which is happening inside," Aretha once said. In 1987, she became the first female artist to be inducted into the Rock & Roll Hall of Fame, paving the way for women of all backgrounds. In 2008, Aretha won her 18th Grammy Award, making her one of the most honoured artists in history, and a symbol of the world's respect.

Want to find out more about **Aretha Franklin?**

Have a read of these great books:

Who was Aretha Franklin? by Nico Medina

A Voice Named Aretha by Katheryn Russell-Brown

Brimming with creative inspiration, how-to projects, and useful information to enrich your everyday life, Quarto Knows is a favourite destination for those pursuing their interests and passions. Visit our site and dig deeper with our books into your area of interest: Quarto Creates, Quarto Cooks, Quarto Homes, Quarto Lives, Quarto Drives, Quarto Explores, Quarto Gifts, or Quarto Kids.

Concept and text © 2020 Maria Isabel Sánchez Vegara. Illustrations © 2020 Amy Blackwell.

First Published in the UK in 2020 by Frances Lincoln Children's Books, an imprint of The Quarto Group.

The Old Brewery, 6 Blundell Street, London N7 9BH, United Kingdom.

T 020 7700 6700 **www.QuartoKnows.com**

First Published in Spain in 2020 under the title Pequeña & Grande Aretha Franklin

by Alba Editorial, s.l.u., Baixada de Sant Miquel, 1, 08002 Barcelona

www.albaeditorial.es

All rights reserved.

Published by arrangement with Alba Editorial, s.l.u. Translation rights arranged by IMC Agència Literària, SL

All rights reserved.

A catalogue record for this book is available from the British Library.

ISBN 978-0-7112-4687-4

Set in Futura BT.

Published by Katie Cotton • Designed by Karissa Santos

Edited by Rachel Williams and Katy Flint • Production by Caragh McAleenan

Manufactured in Guangdong, China CC082020

9 7 5 3 2 4 6 8

Photographic acknowledgements (pages 28-29, from left to right) 1. c. 1960: Studio portrait of American singer Aretha Franklin, wearing a beaded top © Hulton Archive via Getty Images. 2. American soul singer Aretha Franklin, c. 1965 © Val Wilmer via Getty Images 3. Aretha Franklin © Ron Galella/Ron Galella Collection via Getty Images 4. Aretha Franklin performs at the the 56th Presidential Inauguration ceremony for Barack Obama as the 44th President of the United States on the west steps of the Capitol on January 20, 2009 © UPI Photo/Pat Benic via Alamy Stock Photo.

Collect the
Little People, BIG DREAMS series:

FRIDA KAHLO

ISBN: 978-1-84780-770-0

COCO CHANEL

ISBN: 978-1-84780-771-7

MAYA ANGELOU

ISBN: 978-1-84780-890-5

AMELIA EARHART

ISBN: 978-1-84780-885-1

AGATHA CHRISTIE
ISBN: 978-1-84780-959-9

MARIE CURIE

ISBN: 978-1-84780-961-2

ROSA PARKS

ISBN: 978-1-78603-017-7

AUDREY HEPBURN

ISBN: 978-1-78603-052-8

EMMELINE PANKHURST

ISBN: 978-1-78603-019-1

ELLA FITZGERALD

ISBN: 978-1-78603-086-3

ADA LOVELACE

ISBN: 978-1-78603-075-7

JANE AUSTEN

ISBN: 978-1-78603-119-8

GEORGIA O'KEEFFE

ISBN: 978-1-78603-121-1

HARRIET TUBMAN

ISBN: 978-1-78603-289-8

ANNE FRANK

ISBN: 978-1-78603-292-8

MOTHER TERESA

ISBN: 978-1-78603-290-4

JOSEPHINE BAKER

ISBN: 978-1-78603-291-1

L. M. MONTGOMERY

ISBN: 978-1-78603-295-9

JANE GOODALL

ISBN: 978-1-78603-294-2

SIMONE DE BEAUVOIR

ISBN: 978-1-78603-293-5

MUHAMMAD ALI

ISBN: 978-1-78603-733-6

STEPHEN HAWKING

ISBN: 978-1-78603-732-9

MARIA MONTESSORI

ISBN: 978-1-78603-753-4

VIVIENNE WESTWOOD

ISBN: 978-1-78603-756-5

MAHATMA GANDHI

ISBN: 978-1-78603-334-5

DAVID BOWIE

ISBN: 978-1-78603-803-6

WILMA RUDOLPH

ISBN: 978-1-78603-750-3

DOLLY PARTON

ISBN: 978-1-78603-759-6

BRUCE LEE

ISBN: 978-1-78603-335-2

RUDOLF NUREYEV

ISBN: 978-1-78603-336-9

ZAHA HADID

ISBN: 978-1-78603-744-2

MARY SHELLEY

ISBN: 978-1-78603-747-3

MARTIN LUTHER KING JR.

ISBN: 978-0-7112-4566-2

DAVID ATTENBOROUGH

ISBN: 978-0-7112-4563-1

ASTRID LINDGREN

ISBN: 978-1-78603-762-6

EVONNE GOOLAGONG

ISBN: 978-0-7112-4585-3

BOB DYLAN

ISBN: 978-0-7112-4674-4

ALAN TURING

ISBN: 978-0-7112-4677-5

BILLIE JEAN KING

ISBN: 978-0-7112-4692-8

GRETA THUNBERG

ISBN: 978-0-7112-5643-9

JESSE OWENS

ISBN: 978-0-7112-4582-2

JEAN-MICHEL BASQUIAT

ISBN: 978-0-7112-4579-2

ARETHA FRANKLIN

ISBN: 978-0-7112-4687-4

CORAZON AQUINO

ISBN: 978-0-7112-4683-6

PELÉ

ISBN: 978-0-7112-4574-7

ERNEST SHACKLETON

ISBN: 978-0-7112-4570-9

STEVE JOBS

ISBN: 978-0-7112-4576-1

AYRTON SENNA

ISBN: 978-0-7112-4671-3

LOUISE BOURGEOIS

ISBN: 978-0-7112-4689-8

ELTON JOHN

ISBN: 978-0-7112-5838-9

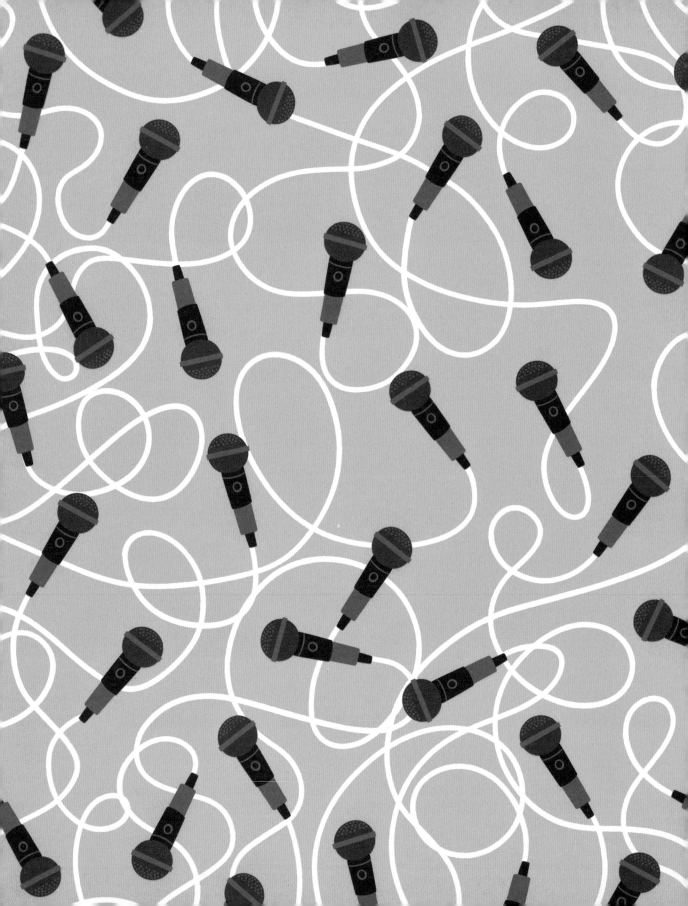